FINDING REST

> Come to me, all who labor and are heavy laden, and I will give you rest. Take my yoke upon you, and learn from me, for I am gentle and lowly in heart, and you will find rest for your souls. For my yoke is easy, and my burden is light.
>
> **MATTHEW 11:28-30**

THE INVITATION

Are you stressed? Does your life seem to be in constant conflict? Do you sometimes feel as if there is a burden on your back—a heaviness in your soul—that continually weighs you down?

If you are struggling to cope with a life that is confusing and out of control, take heart. If you are searching for rest for your soul, there is good news. Jesus is offering a personal invitation to you.

WHY IS REST SO DIFFICULT TO FIND?

The work of this world always seems more important than Jesus's invitation in Matthew 11:28. Even though you desire to give your heart and mind a break, it is nearly impossible to turn away from the priorities set in place by the culture you live in.

4. Although you deserve to die for your own sins, Jesus Christ (who never sinned) died for you. He was your substitute. He made the payment for your sins when he died on the cross and rose again.

"Christ died for our sins . . . he was buried . . . he was raised on the third day in accordance with the Scriptures."
(1 Corinthians 15:3-4)

5. You must place your trust, not in anything good you have done or will do, but only in what Christ has already done for you.

"For God so loved the world, that he gave his only Son, that whoever believes in him should not perish but have eternal life." *(John 3:16)*

6. You cannot earn eternal life; it is a gift that you either accept or reject. When you receive God's gift, you become his child, and you are adopted into his family.

"But to all who did receive him, who believed in his name, he gave the right to become children of God." *(John 1:12)*

If you've already trusted Christ as your Savior, here are some things you can do to grow in your relationship with him:

- Read the Bible to learn more about God and his plan for your life.

- Pray to God often to share your joys and problems and to confess your sins.

- Attend a Bible-teaching church where you can worship God and get to know other Christians.

- Share your faith. You have just received a wonderful gift. Tell someone!

To read the Bible, learn about Jesus, or find a church in your area, visit **Crossway.org/LearnMore**.

www.goodnewstracts.org

Bible references: ESV. Written by Gretchen Fant.